THE L G B T Q+
GUIDE TO BEATING BULLYING™

Working with Your School to Create a Safe Environment

Avery Elizabeth Hurt

Rosen
YA
New York

For all LGBTQ+ kids. It will get better.

Published in 2018 by The Rosen Publishing Group, Inc.
29 East 21st Street, New York, NY 10010

First Edition

Library of Congress Cataloging-in-Publication Data

Names: Hurt, Avery Elizabeth, author.
Title: Working with your school to create a safe environment / Avery Elizabeth Hurt.
Description: New York : Rosen Publishing, 2018 | Series: The LQBTQ+ guide to beating bullying | Includes bibliographical references and index. | Audience: Grades 7–12.
Identifiers: LCCN 2017002783 | ISBN 9781508174356 (library-bound) | ISBN 9781508174332 (pbk.) | ISBN 9781508174349 (6-pack)
Subjects: LCSH: Bullying in schools—Prevention—Juvenile literature. | School safety—Juvenile literature.
Classification: LCC LB3013.3 .W64 2018 | DDC 371.5/8—dc23
LC record available at https://lccn.loc.gov/2017002783

Manufactured in the United States of America

CONTENTS

INTRODUCTION

In 2015, the US Supreme Court ruled in *Obergefell v. Hodges* that the Constitution guarantees the right of same-sex couples to marry. In celebration, the White House and government buildings around the country were illuminated with rainbow colors (a symbol of LGBTQ+ pride) on the evening the decision was declared. It was clear that attitudes toward LGBTQ+ people were changing. This landmark ruling followed a series of successes for LGBTQ+ rights. In 2005, Canada became the first country outside of Europe to legalize gay marriage. In

The White House was lit up in the colors of the LGBTQ+ pride flag in celebration of the 2015 Supreme Court decision legalizing gay marriage in the United States.

2011, "Don't Ask, Don't Tell," which banned gays and lesbians from serving openly in the US military, was overturned, and by 2016 almost half of the LGBTQ+ population lived in states that prohibited bullying on the basis of sexual orientation and gender identity.

Despite the cause for celebration, homophobia still exists, and many states continue to pass discriminatory laws. For example, there are laws that allow businesses to refuse service to LGBTQ+ customers and laws that require transgender people to use the restroom that matches the gender assigned to them at birth, rather than the gender they identify as.

School is also not a safe place for many LGBTQ+ youth. In a 2016 survey of high school students, the Centers for Disease Control and Prevention (CDC) found that 34.2 percent of gay, lesbian, and bisexual students, and 24.9 percent of students who were not sure of their sexual identity, had been bullied on school property. The same survey found that 23 percent of LGBTQ+ students had been victims of sexual violence, and 30 percent had attempted suicide sometime during the prior twelve months. Clearly, there is still a lot of work to do to make schools a safe and welcoming place for LGBTQ+ students.

In 2010, after the suicides of several LGBTQ+ teens, columnist Dan Savage and his husband, Terry Miller, began a project called It Gets Better. The project is designed to reassure LGBTQ+ young people that even though they may be enduring rough times now, life does get better—often much better—once they are out of school and in the wider world. LGBTQ+ people from all walks of life made videos sharing their stories of school bullying and how they survived while in school and thrived in life after school. The straight community, including President Barack Obama and Secretary of State Hillary Clinton, contributed messages of hope and support.

However, wouldn't it be great if things were to get better *now*?

Wouldn't it be wonderful if LGBTQ+ people didn't have to begin their adult lives with the emotional—and sometimes physical—scars from the treatment they received throughout their school years? This text is here to help you understand that it *can* get better now. By working with teachers, administrators, and peers, both LGBTQ+ and straight, you can make your school a safe and welcoming place for all students.

CHAPTER ONE

TARGETED BULLYING

Bullying can take many forms. It can include insults and taunting, spreading rumors and gossiping, and even acts of physical violence. When experts define bullying, they typically use at least two criteria: The bully must intend to either physically or emotionally harm the victim, and, perhaps most importantly, there has to be an imbalance of power between the bully and the victim. Bullies harass people who aren't in a position to do anything about it. The imbalance of power is sometimes physical (the bully is bigger and stronger than the victim), but it can often be a kind of social power—where the bully is in a position to deny victims admission to clubs or groups. For example, the bully is on a sports team and athletes are revered at school and in the community, or the bully is in a popular clique and the victim is not.

Choosing Targets

Anyone who is different, or perceived to be different, from the dominant group can become a target for bullies. Students who are lesbian, gay, bisexual, transgender, or are in the process of questioning their sexual identity—a group of people known as LGBTQ+—are targeted more often than other teens. According to the 2013 National School Climate Survey, conducted by the Gay, Lesbian and Straight Education Network (GLSEN), appearance is the most common reason for bullying, but being LGBTQ+ or being perceived as LGBTQ+ comes in at number two. Until LGBTQ+ people are more fully accepted by society, they are likely to remain a favorite target of the bullies of the world.

There's no doubt that being bullied hurts. But often the safest and most effective way to handle the situation is simply to walk away.

When bullies go after LGBTQ+ people, they often use demeaning words and hurtful characterizations. Whoever said that words can't hurt you never experienced bullying. But words aren't the only weapons bullies use against their victims. Sometimes, they use physical force and even real weapons. While the 2016 CDC survey of high school students points out that most LGBTQ+ youth are happy and thriving during adolescence, it also demonstrates that they are at a far greater risk of violence than straight and cisgender teens.

THE RIGHT WORDS

Bullies use a lot of demeaning words for LGBTQ+ people. Here is the proper way to reference those who are LGBTQ+:

Asexual: A person who is not interested in sexual activity with any person.

Bisexual: A person who is sexually attracted to men and women.

Cisgender: A person whose gender identity matches the gender they were assigned at birth.

Gay: A person who is sexually attracted primarily to people of the same sex; this term can be used for men and women, but often lesbian is used for women.

Gender nonconforming: A person who does not fit other people's stereotypes of how a person of a particular gender should dress or behave.

Heterosexual: A person who is sexually attracted primarily to people of the opposite sex.

Lesbian: A woman who is sexually attracted primarily to other women.

Pansexual: Someone who is sexually attracted to a person regardless of that person's biological gender or gender identity.

Queer: A catch-all term that refers to people with nontraditional gender identities or sexual orientations. Bullies often use it in an offensive way, but many LGBTQ+ people embrace the term.

Questioning: A person who is questioning and exploring their sexual orientation or gender identity.

Transgender: A person who does not identify with the gender they were assigned at birth and who may or may not have undergone sex reassignment surgery and/or hormonal therapy, as well as people who live their lives as someone of a different gender from their birth gender.

When Bullies Whisper

Some of the most devastating forms of bullying are subtle and hard for others to notice or even recognize as bullying. When someone refuses to use the right pronouns for a transgender person, that's bullying. When someone uses the word "gay" to mean "lame" or "stupid," and then insists they're just joking and it's your problem for being so sensitive, that's bullying. When you're excluded from groups or not picked for sports teams, even though you're as good as everyone else, that's bullying. When you're

Teens who are being bullied can often feel lonely when they sit by themselves in the lunchroom or are left on the sidelines during school sports events.

ignored in meetings or conversations in the lunchroom, that's bullying. Although these bullies may not be making fun of you directly, or using or threatening violence, these are still forms of bullying.

In some ways, subtle bullying may be worse than obvious examples. This type of bullying is easier to normalize than the more overt kind, and it is easier to blame victims for being overly sensitive or troublemakers when they complain about it. More subtle forms of bullying can often pass under the radar, and the fact that some people who engage in this type of bullying may not acknowledge or even realize what they are doing makes it harder to address.

Bullies in Cyberspace

Bullying is not limited to one-on-one encounters. When bullies use electronic technology to do their bullying, it's called cyberbullying. Cyberbullying is increasingly common. A 2013 Youth Risk Behavior Surveillance Survey by the CDC found that 15 percent of students in grades nine to twelve had been cyberbullied.

Cyberbullies post mean comments, embarrassing pictures, and even fake profiles on social media sites. They hound their victims with nasty texts and emails. When a bully posts something rude about you on Facebook, everyone sees it. The relative anonymity of social media can also bring out the bully in people who normally keep such tendencies under wraps. The effects of cyberbullying are similar to bullying that takes place in person,

Speaking up in class or concentrating on schoolwork can be especially hard for teens who are dealing with bullies at school.

but because the potential audience is much greater and the information posted can be difficult to delete permanently, the reach of cyberbullies is much greater. Social media can be great for LGBTQ+ people, providing a community that may be hard to find locally, but it also makes it easier for bullies to do damage.

The Dangers of Bullying

Some people think that bullying is a normal part of growing up and that kids bully each other from time to time until everyone eventually grows out of it. Facts show otherwise. According to the CDC, victims of bullying—particularly LGBTQ+ bullying—are far more likely than other kids to commit or attempt suicide, and lesbian, gay, and bisexual youth in grades seven to twelve are more than twice as likely to attempt suicide than kids who aren't LGBTQ+. These are the worst, but not only, consequences of bullying. According to GSLEN's 2013 National School Climate Survey, kids who are bullied are more likely than other kids to suffer from depression, anxiety, and a variety of other health problems. They are more likely to abuse alcohol and drugs, and fall behind in schoolwork and fail to meet academic or life goals.

Bullying should never be ignored or dismissed as some kind of rite of passage. Even when bullying is not physical, it is still an act of violence. A school where bullying is allowed is a school that promotes a climate of fear and disrespect.

CHAPTER TWO

BANISHING BULLIES

In her speech at the 2016 Democratic National Convention, First Lady Michelle Obama said that her family has a motto when "someone is cruel or acts like a bully": "When they go low, we go high." Teens don't have to stoop to the level of bullies to stand up for themselves.

When students—LGBTQ+ or not—stand up to bullies, they need support. Taking a stand may be especially difficult for kids who are LGBTQ+ but not out, or those who are figuring out their own sexual orientation and don't want any unwanted attention in the process. Still, it's very important to show bullies that they aren't going to get support from the rest of the school. Standing up to bullies doesn't mean starting or being lured into a fight. It does mean refusing to give up self-respect and respect for others.

Standing up to bullies can be as simple as holding your head up and looking the bully in the eye. It's never a good idea to respond with anger or aggression, but firmness can be effective. Responding with phrases such as "Knock it off," "I'm fine with the way I am," or "That wasn't funny. That was mean" shows bullies they are not getting to you without increasing the conflict.

Of course, if the situation seems dangerous, walking away is the best thing to do. The next step is to tell a trusted teacher or other adult. Never let bullying go unreported, even the small stuff. If small incidents are ignored, the bullying will likely intensify. It's important for kids to be able to stand up for themselves,

Asking teachers and school administrators for help may make you uncomfortable at first, but it is one of the best strategies to reduce bullying in schools.

but it is not their job alone. Teachers and school administrators must work together to keep kids safe. They can't do that if they don't know what's going on.

Be Proactive

There are plenty of ways to be proactive about preventing bullying. Offer to serve on a safety committee, or organize one if it doesn't exist already. Develop an anonymous reporting system where kids who are bullied or who observe bullying can report it without fear of retaliation. Ask permission to post anti-bullying posters around the school. Some schools may even allow posters that promote a positive attitude toward LGBTQ+ people. Educating about LGBTQ+ issues doesn't require coming out yourself. Straight and cisgender teens, and LGBTQ+ teens who are not out, can do a lot to combat bullying. They can speak about LGBTQ+ issues and anti-bullying programs at PTA meetings and school assemblies. They can do school projects on LGBTQ+ leaders, educators, and historical figures.

Students who aren't comfortable talking publicly about LGBTQ+ issues can talk about bullying in general. The more teachers, parents, and administrators know what is going on in the classrooms and hallways of their schools, the better they can develop guidelines and programs to prevent bullying in the first place. Many civil rights organizations—including the Human Rights Campaign (HRC); American Civil Liberties Union (ACLU); and Southern Poverty Law Center (SPLC), through its project Teaching Tolerance—work to support the civil rights of

Actor and television host Mario Lopez is surrounded by students at the STOMP OUT Bullying Pep Rally in New Rochelle, NY. These kinds of events help educate school communities about LGBTQ+ bullying.

all people, regardless of their race, socioeconomic status, sexual orientation, or gender identity. These organizations have resources for educating your school and community.

Getting to Know You

Marriage equality is only part of the picture of LGBTQ+ rights, but it is an indicator of changing views about LGBTQ+ people.

There are important lessons to be learned from how this victory for LGBTQ+ rights came to be. Many were astonished at how quickly the barriers to same-sex marriage came tumbling down in the United States. According to data journalist Nate Silver, in 2004, 31 percent of Americans supported gay marriage. Just ten years later, that figure was up to 57 percent. Silver explains that such a rapid change in opinion could not be due to a generational change. It happened because *individuals* changed their minds.

Many LGBTQ+ rights activists think the main reason for the rapid public acceptance of marriage equality was that as more straight and cisgender people got to know LGBTQ+ people— the more they went to school with them, played sports with them, and sat at the dinner table with them—the more they realized LGBTQ+ people aren't all that different. They are just people like everyone else, and they deserve to be treated with dignity and respect.

If LGBTQ+ right activists are correct in that the acceptance of same-sex marriage was due in large measure to straight and cisgender people getting to know LGBTQ+ people, then it seems to follow that when kids who aren't LGBTQ+ get to know their LGBTQ+ classmates, it may become easier to reduce bullying in school. The more people are open about their sexual orientation and gender identity, the more quickly LGBTQ+ people become part of mainstream culture. Therefore, they become a less desirable targets for bullies.

However, for many LGBTQ+ teens, coming out is not an option. It may be that they are afraid their parents will

The rapid change in the American public's attitude toward gay marriage may bode well for the future of LGBTQ+ rights in other areas of life.

disapprove, or they may not be ready to tell their friends. In addition, many young people are still exploring their sexual orientation and gender identity and may not be ready to discuss these matters publicly. The decision to come out is a personal one, and it should never be made lightly. An individual's decision about the right time to come out must be respected. That's why LGBTQ+ teens who are already out can serve as ambassadors for the rest of the LGBTQ+ community.

MYTHS AND FACTS

Myth: Bullies are always at the top of the pecking order.

Fact: While bullies are sometimes the alpha dogs of the school, it's likely that they are also the victims of abuse, perhaps at home or in some other setting. When people are physically, verbally, or emotionally abused, they often take it out on someone else.

Myth: Stopping bullying in schools won't do any good because it will still be prevalent online.

Fact: According to StopBullying.gov (https://www.stop bullying.gov), the US government's anti-bullying campaign, cyberbullying often starts in person, then migrates online. When bullying is addressed in schools, it is less likely to happen online.

Myth: When bullies call you "gay" or "queer," it always means they are taunting you about your sexual orientation.

Fact: Some kids don't even have a clear understanding of what it means to be LGBTQ+. They may just be throwing words around to see if they can get under your skin. If you're questioning your sexual orientation or gender identity, don't assume the bully's taunts have much to do with that process.

CHAPTER THREE

ALLIES ARE OUT THERE

Being an LGBTQ+ teen can make you feel lonelier than you thought possible. According to the American Academy of Pediatrics, an estimated 10 percent of high school students are either LGBTQ+ or questioning. That means if there are 1,000 people in your high school, roughly 90 of them are LGBTQ+. That's enough to fill at least three homerooms. Spread throughout an entire school, though, it's not that many students. LGBTQ+ kids may be a very small group.

Even if you are the only LGBTQ+ kid in your class, don't lose hope. Acceptance of LGBTQ+ people is increasing at a fast rate. According to Gallup's 2016 Mood of the Nation survey, 60 percent of Americans are satisfied with the acceptance of gays and lesbians in the United States. That's up from 53 percent in 2015 and 32 percent in 2006. In addition, the number of young people who are supportive of LGBTQ+ rights is even greater. A 2016 GenForward Survey of young Americans found that people between the ages eighteen and thirty supported LGBTQ+ rights in percentages ranging from 80 to 92. This means that allies are out there.

Reading the Signs

There are ways to tell if someone is an LGBTQ+ ally or might easily be persuaded to join the cause of LGBTQ+ rights. Rainbow flags and marriage equality bumper stickers speak for themselves,

If a teen has allies on their side, it can be easier to resist bullies. Just because an ally might be a bit awkward when first talking about LGBTQ+ issues doesn't mean they can't be a great source of support.

but allies and potential allies often show subtler signs of support. People who read LGBTQ+-themed books or do reports on LGBTQ+ writers or historical figures are potential allies. A potential ally might mention an item about LGBTQ+ issues they've read in the news—and discuss it in a positive way. Perhaps they talk about having another friend or a relative who is LGBTQ+. Even if their comments seem a little clumsy (perhaps especially when they seem clumsy), they are often attempts to let LGBTQ+ teens know that someone is on their side.

Joining in with other groups that are working for social, economic, or environmental justice can be a great way to gain allies and help others at the same time.

People who are involved in other progressive causes are likely to be sympathetic to the needs of LGBTQ+ people as well. People who speak out about racial or socioeconomic injustice are often also aware of, and keen to put a stop to, LGBTQ+ bullying and discrimination. Seek out students who are active in social justice and environmental groups.

Sometimes, it's not what people say but how they say it that lets LGBTQ+ teens know they have an ally in the making. When someone makes an effort to use gender neutral language—using terms like "partner" or "companion"— and gets the terminology right, saying "sexual orientation" rather than "sexual preference," that's a good sign that they are a potential ally.

Not everyone is comfortable standing up to bullies, but teens who seem uncomfortable or offended—or even leave the scene— when LGBTQ+ kids are being bullied are possible allies. They obviously don't like what's going on, and with a little education and support from other kids (both LGBTQ+ and straight), they can go from being passive supporters to active allies.

Allies Need Help, Too

As wonderful as allies may be, and as great as it is to have them, even the most well-meaning straight and cisgender person doesn't always get where LGBTQ+ people are coming from. Help them understand. Try to be as patient and understanding with your allies as you want them to be with you.

For some, learning that a friend or classmate is LGBTQ+ can be distressing at first. The ally may not even be upset that their friend has come out as LGBTQ+. They may just need time to adjust to their friend's LGBTQ+ identity. Be patient as they come to terms with what may seem like a new you. The more supportive you are of their effort to develop a deeper understanding of your LGBTQ+ identity, the more supportive they're likely to be of your struggle for your rights. It's easier for allies to stand up to a bully when they know the person they're standing up for has their backs, too, even if it's in a different way.

GIVING THANKS

Coming out as LGBTQ+ can be hard. But for some people, coming out as an LGBTQ+ ally can be difficult, too. It's great when LGBTQ+ people support allies who may risk being targeted by bullies themselves. Something as simple as saying "Thanks for the post" to a classmate who has posted a rainbow flag or positive message on their Facebook page could mean a lot. When someone goes out of their way to stand up to a bully, a thank-you note slipped into a locker or between the pages of a textbook might make the student feel it was worthwhile to take that risk.

Talk About It

Allies may be perfectly willing to help but not know what to do. Preventing bullying isn't just about standing up to bullying when you see it. It's about creating an atmosphere where bullying can't thrive. Allies may need a little—or maybe a lot—of help from LGBTQ+ peers in order to be good allies.

Just because some people are uncomfortable with LGBTQ+ people doesn't necessarily mean they are anti-LGBTQ+ or can't be good allies. They may be uncomfortable or awkward if they have never knowingly been around LGBTQ+ people before.

They don't want to say anything that might come across as dumb or offensive. Sometimes, when friends learn that you are LGBTQ+, they have a lot of questions. This is understandable. However, LGBTQ+ people should not feel obligated to give anyone any more information or details about their lives than they are willing to give.

Not everyone understands the challenges that LGBTQ+ teens face. Educating allies allows them to be there for you and is an important part of coming out.

It's fine to explain that you are comfortable with only so much sharing. Though it is all too obvious to LGBTQ+ people, those who are straight and cisgender may not realize the kinds of difficulties that LGBTQ+ people face. A big part of having allies is educating them. If you're out to only a few people, be sure your allies know this and that they understand the importance of letting you come out in your own way and at your own pace. No one wants an overzealous ally to accidentally out them before they are ready.

Straight allies are essential to eliminating bullying in school. But LGBTQ+ people need to be allies for each other, too. Transgender people may have the hardest road when it comes to societal acceptance and staying safe in school. Supporting transgender people is a great way to demonstrate what it means to be a strong ally.

CHAPTER FOUR

MAKE IT OFFICIAL: START A GSA

A Gay-Straight Alliance (GSA) is an excellent way to encourage straight allies to join LGBTQ+ students in transforming the culture of a school. A GSA is an official, student-run club, just like a chess club or a drama club. GSAs serve several functions. They are a great place for LGBTQ+ students to get together, get to know one another, and provide

GSAs can help students take a stand against bullying, but they're also a great way to make friends and have fun. Events such as parties and cookouts go a long way toward developing a sense of community.

support for each other. They can be especially useful for kids who are questioning their sexual orientation and/or gender identity and need a safe place to talk, ask questions, and be themselves.

GSAs aren't just for the LGBTQ+ students. They offer a welcoming space for allies to get to know LGBTQ+ classmates and learn about the challenges their peers face. GSA-sponsored events, such as cookouts, movie nights, and parties, provide opportunities for people to have fun together, which is one of the best ways to build community. Watching and discussing LGBTQ+-themed movies, or starting a LGBTQ+ book club, can combine education, consciousness-raising, and entertainment.

There is more to a GSA than socializing, however. A well-run and active GSA can educate and advocate for change. Because it is officially a school organization, a GSA has the legitimacy to speak up for LGBTQ+ causes and promote programs and initiatives, such as an anti-bullying task force or an anonymous tip line where students can report any bullying they've witnessed.

The Small Print

To start a GSA at your school, you must meet certain guidelines. Find out what these guidelines are and follow them exactly. A GSA can be a powerful tool for change, so avoid getting off on the wrong foot with the school administration. The GSA may be required to write a constitution for the organization. Even if that's not required, it's a good idea to put together a set of bylaws that govern how the organization will be run. This will cover

Getting involved in writing the constitution of a GSA can be great training for a career and for lifelong participation in various forms of political activism.

things like how officers are elected, when and where meetings can be held, and how funds are raised and managed. If this is all new to you, ask another organization at your school how they structured their group. Or go to GLSEN (http://www.glsen.org) to find out more about how to get started.

Choosing the right faculty advisor for a GSA can make forming the club much more rewarding. A teacher who is there to guide you can also smooth relations with the administration.

The Perfect Faculty Advisor

A GSA will almost certainly need a faculty advisor, and since this person will be the group's liaison with the school administration, give careful thought to this choice. The ideal person is one who is already supportive of LGBTQ+ rights. Teachers who have stood up for LGBTQ+ students when they were being bullied, or those who include LGBTQ+ people and issues in their lessons, are obvious choices. But if none are obvious, a little observation might offer some clues. It's not unlike watching for signs from allies. Teachers typically keep their politics out of the classroom, but they give subtle signals about how they really feel. Look for marriage equality bumper stickers on a teacher's car or indications that a teacher supports other progressive causes. A teacher who seems sensitive to women's issues, for example, might be sensitive to LGBTQ+ issues as well.

Straight allies might be concerned that others will think they are LGBTQ+ if they join a GSA. These concerns can be alleviated by making it clear in the group's bylaws that no assumption about sexual orientation or gender identity is implied by membership in the GSA or attendance at its events. A similar statement can be printed on invitations, announcements, and posters about GSA events. Pretty soon, the GSA will have a character of its own, and as the student body gets familiar with the group and the activities it sponsors, those concerns will diminish.

WHAT'S IN A NAME?

Choosing a name for your new club can be fun—and challenging. Your school may impose restrictions, so be sure to find out what, if any, rules apply. Even if there are no rules about names, a school that is on the conservative side might be touchy about names that are too edgy or humorous. One benefit of a GSA is working within the system to bring people together and create a more inclusive environment. Upsetting the school administration is not a good strategy.

That doesn't mean you can't have fun. A Catholic college in Spokane, Washington, did not allow use of the words "gay" or "homosexual" in organization names, so the founders of a GSA there came up with the name HERO, an acronym for Helping to Educate Regarding Orientation. Another GSA is called READI, which stands for Rainbow Education Alliance of Diverse Individuals.

Members of a GSA can play around with terms such as "pride" or "queer," but keep in mind that you want your club to appeal to everyone, not just LGBTQ+ students. Some students who aren't totally comfortable with supporting the LGBTQ+ community might find it easier to learn about LGBTQ+ issues and get to know LGBTQ+ students better if the name of the group is a little more subtle. Also, a name that takes some explaining (an acronym like HERO, for example) could be a great opportunity to start a discussion about being LGBTQ+. As your efforts pay off and your school becomes more accepting of LGBTQ+ students, you can be less careful about what terms you use in your promotional materials.

Don't Take No for an Answer

A GSA is designed to bring students together, promote understanding, and end LGBTQ+ bullying. These goals should be high on the list of your school's priorities as well. However, that doesn't mean the administration is going to be on board right away. According to the ACLU, schools sometimes resist the idea. Some teachers and school administrations may have never heard of a GSA and be confused about its mission. Or they may fear the club is intended to promote an LGBTQ+ "lifestyle," "recruit" teens to be LGBTQ+, or even cause students to question their gender identities. Don't let attitudes like these dampen your enthusiasm.

One of the main purposes of a GSA is to educate people so that they won't have these ideas, but to get the club going, a little diplomacy may be required. When presenting the idea to the administration, be sure to emphasize that the benefits of a GSA apply to the entire student body and that the goal of the club is to prevent bullying by encouraging inclusiveness and acceptance of all gender identities and sexual orientations. When it comes down to it, though, don't take no for an answer. According to the Equal Access Act of 1984, if a secondary school allows any other extracurricular clubs and organizations, it has to allow the formation of a GSA.

As founding members of a GSA, you are now among your school's leaders. This is an honor and a responsibility. Simply starting a GSA at your school won't stop bullying—you'll have to work hard for that. But it will add a measure of legitimacy to the school's LGBTQ+ community.

CHAPTER FIVE

GET IT ON THE BOOKS: FROM ACTIVISM TO SCHOOL POLICY

It might not feel like it at times, but LGBTQ+ students who attend public school have rights. You need to know what those rights are. A federal law called Title IX requires public

LGBTQ+ teens may have to be assertive to ensure that their legal rights are respected by the students, faculty, and administration of their school.

schools to address the harassment of LGBTQ+ students the same way they would address the harassment of anyone else.

In addition, under the Second Amendment of the US Constitution, LGBTQ+ students have the right to express their identity. They can wear clothes or cut their hair in a way that matches their gender identity, even if it is different from the gender assigned to them at birth. It is illegal for other students or teachers to harass LGBTQ+ students or treat them differently because of who they are. Some people use their religious beliefs as an excuse to bully others, but having different beliefs is not an excuse to bully or harass someone.

Schools have the right to establish dress codes, but they must be enforced equally. If a school allows students to wear T-shirts with political or cultural slogans, they can't keep students

Kaleigh Colson, president of Portland High School's Gay-Straight-Trans Alliance in Portland, Maine, shows her colors as she gets ready for the city's Gay Pride Parade.

from wearing T-shirts that express LGBTQ+ identity, such as a Pride T-shirt. The school can't forbid students from talking about being LGBTQ+. Teachers can control what subjects they teach in class, but they can't prevent students from talking about being LGBTQ+ or discussing LGBTQ+ issues at lunch or in the halls between classes. If LGBTQ+ students are being bullied at school, the school has a legal responsibility to take action.

Making a Report

When an LGBTQ+ student is bullied—even if that bullying is done by a teacher—the student must report it to a counselor or principal at the school. This will give the school a chance to address concerns, and it will ensure that the incident and the complaint are on record. Victims of bullying should give a detailed report of exactly what happened, including dates, times, and places, and keep a copy of this information for themselves.

If you think your rights are being violated, but you aren't sure or are afraid to speak up, get in touch with the ACLU or SPLC, two organizations that can offer guidance when navigating issues around bullying

The laws aren't as clear when it comes to the use of locker rooms and bathrooms by transgender students. There are questions about how schools should deal with names on the records of trans students and if schools are required to use the pronouns of the gender that a trans student identifies with.

Schools and the courts are tackling these issues. In 2016, North Carolina passed HB2, the "bathroom bill" that requires

YOUNG LOBBYISTS

Think there's not much you can do because you're "just a student"? Don't be so sure. In 1993, Massachusetts became the first state to pass a law, called the Gay and Lesbian Student Rights Law, prohibiting discrimination in public schools on the basis of sexual orientation. To get this landmark legislation passed, thousands of students, both LGBTQ+ and straight, wrote letters, attended rallies, met with state representatives, and spoke at venues statewide. These students shared information about the legislation, as well as their personal stories of being bullied and treated unjustly because of their sexual orientation. The law was passed because the young people it protected worked hard to make it happen.

trans students to use the bathroom that matches the gender they were assigned at birth, rather than the gender they identify with. A trans student challenged this law, and the case is still working its way through the courts.

Shortly after North Carolina's "bathroom bill" was passed, the Obama administration directed schools to allow students to use the bathroom that corresponds with their gender identity or else lose federal funding. After the Obama administration took this action, more than twenty states filed lawsuits challenging the directive. After Donald J. Trump took office in 2017, he reversed the directive put forth by the Obama administration.

Schools should be dedicated to educating and protecting all students, and in most cases, teachers and administrators will be in your corner. Just be sure to know your rights, and when you have a complaint, bring it up respectfully—but do bring it up.

Keeping Up with Policy

Policies change frequently as new laws are passed and existing laws are challenged. To be well informed about LGBTQ+ rights and what can be done if these rights are violated, LGBTQ+ students need to keep up with the changing political landscape. All citizens should be informed about their governments, national and local. However, it is more crucial for LGBTQ+ people to stay abreast of law and policy changes. Many LGBTQ+ teens don't know that they have legal protection from bullies. Such policies didn't just come into being. Many people worked hard to put these protections in place, and plenty of people are continuing to work to strengthen them and make sure that LGBTQ+ rights aren't taken away.

Speaking up when your rights are in jeopardy is essential. However, students don't have to wait until something bad happens to get involved. By taking part in their communities, young people—both LGBTQ+ and their allies—can shape their local governments and their schools to create a better and safer

Presenting your case in support of LGBTQ+ rights to school boards and community organizations will feel less overwhelming if you've done plenty of preparation.

environment for LGBTQ+ people. A citizen doesn't have to be old enough to vote to influence legislation.

National organizations such as the Human Rights Campaign, which works to achieve full equality for LGBTQ+ people, offer ways to get involved in issues affecting LGBTQ+ rights. Many of these organizations have local chapters. Often, the best place to start is your neighborhood. Policies and procedures in your school are likely decided by the local school board. High school students are too young to serve on school boards, but they are not too young to write letters and talk to board members. If their parents support LGBTQ+ rights, they might encourage them to run for school board. A good way to keep up with laws that affect different schools is to visit the National School Boards Association website (http://www.nsba.org).

10 GREAT QUESTIONS TO ASK AN LGBTQ+ ACTIVIST

1. What can I do if I think my school is violating federal law but am afraid that if I say anything, the bullying will get worse?

2. I think there are teachers at my school who support ending the bullying of LGBTQ+ kids. How do I approach them without risking retaliation from a teacher in case I'm wrong?

3. There are very few LGBTQ+ kids at my school. How can so few of us make a difference?

4. Can clubs and sports teams at my school make rules based on religious beliefs that prevent LGBTQ+ students from joining?

5. Where can I turn for help if I have been physically attacked by bullies at school, but the administration hasn't done enough to stop it?

6. What can I do if one of the biggest bullies at school is a teacher?

7. How can I help LGBTQ+ students who are being bullied when I'm afraid to speak up because I fear speaking up will out me and I'm not ready for that?

8. Some friends and I are thinking of starting a GSA, but wouldn't it be a bully magnet?

9. The school administration is blocking our efforts to start a GSA. I know they are legally required to allow it, but how can I get them to recognize our rights?

10. Can kids who aren't LGBTQ+ join national organizations that are working for LGBTQ+ rights?

CHAPTER SIX

IT TAKES A VILLAGE

Think for a moment about people who have changed the world: Martin Luther King Jr., John F. Kennedy, Mahatma Gandhi. What do they have in common? They were brave and determined, certainly. But perhaps the most striking trait they share is they were good communicators. We remember the soaring oratory of Dr. King's sermons, the moving rhetoric of Kennedy's speeches, and the quiet power of Gandhi's words.

Much of the work of changing the world was done behind the scenes. These leaders knew not only how to encourage and inspire millions, but also how to frame their arguments and make a case for their agendas. Perhaps most important, they knew how to listen. For every stirring speech, there were hundreds of quiet meetings and phone calls and one-on-one conversations.

To change the culture—and policies and practices—of a school, you'll need to persuade not only your fellow students, but also teachers, administrators, and members of the school board and community. That will take an entire range of communication skills, and you will have to use them in a variety of settings, from the podium to the negotiating table.

On August 28, 1963, more than 200,000 people gathered on the Mall in Washington, DC, to hear Martin Luther King Jr. give his now-famous "I Have a Dream" speech.

FINDING SUCCESS

There are steps necessary for a successful negotiation. These steps include the following:

1) Do your homework. Have all the information and sources at your fingertips. Instead of saying, "LGBTQ+ kids are frequently targeted by bullies," present the government report that shows they are.

2) Before the meeting begins, know the issues and concerns of the people you are negotiating with. Don't let this knowledge keep you from listening to what they say. Not only may you learn something, you will be showing respect for those on the other side of the issue. Give them time to state their case, too.

3) Immediately establish common ground—in this case, the desire for a better school. Then discuss how to get there using words like "we" and "our."

4) Be willing to give up some demands, but don't give up too much. Always look for trade-offs. If you have to make a concession, ask for something in return.

5) Don't be emotional. This is a very emotional issue, but the negotiating table is not the place to express that.

The Other Side of the Table

It seems so obvious. Bullying is unacceptable. LGBTQ+ students need and deserve to be treated with respect, just like everyone else. An environment where students are kind and accepting of one another is essential to a productive learning environment, as well as to a world worth living in. So why is it so hard to convince people to do what it takes to ensure that schools are bully-free zones for LGBTQ+ kids?

People usually don't resist the big goals: equality, justice, peace. They resist the steps it takes to get there. Despite passage of the Equal Access Act, school boards faced with approving an application to start a GSA can be hesitant to approve the request. This is not because they are determined to make life miserable for LGBTQ+ students, but because they are concerned that they will get negative feedback from parents, or they are worried that the club will exacerbate trouble between groups of students. They may resist anonymous tip boxes because of concerns that unsupported accusations might leave them in the awkward position between respecting the rights of the victim and the rights of the accused. To make the case for any goal, people who are working for change must understand the reasons for resistance.

Understanding the challenges faced by the people on the other side of the table is essential to addressing and getting beyond resistance. In other words, you have to listen to what people are saying, even when you think they are wrong. Then you have to reframe your argument in a way that addresses their concerns as well as your goals. Sometimes, you have to compromise. For example, they may be more comfortable with a GSA if you don't use LGBTQ+ in the name. Even with the Equal Access Act, school boards are allowed to have a say in the name. But that's a small compromise for all the progress you've gained.

Making the Case

Sometimes, the most obvious argument is not the most effective one. There is overwhelming scientific evidence that smoking causes cancer and heart disease, cutting years off the lives of

To be an effective activist you need to craft your message carefully. While not everyone can be as brilliant a speaker as Martin Luther King Jr., LGBTQ+ teens should use clear and concise language to state their cause.

smokers. Yet anti-smoking advocates have found that pointing out that smoking can interfere with athletic performance and make skin wrinkly is much more effective than pointing out that it can kill you. It seems like a no-brainer to point out to teachers and administrators that life will be vastly better for LGBTQ+ students if they implement anti-bullying measures. But it might be better to point out how much easier it will be for the administration to run the school if the school is safer and more welcoming to all students. This doesn't mean giving up the desire to have anti-bullying measures in place. It means framing the

During a school board meeting in San Diego, California, PTA member Kelly Barnes and her nine-year-old son Simon Bye hold signs supporting a transgender student's right to use the boys' locker room.

argument in a way that gets the attention of the people you are trying to win over while also appealing to their self-interest.

Of course, arguments designed to show the benefits of an LGBTQ+ safe school aren't the stuff of T-shirt slogans and posters. These are the kinds of arguments you make in meetings and letters. There is a place for both. First, you appeal to the emotions, then you close the deal with the facts and policy details. A poster showing data that schools with vigorous anti-bullying policies have higher graduation rates than those that don't isn't going to inspire many people to join the cause. But this kind of data will be priceless when you sit down at the table with the school administration or local school board to explain why an anti-bullying task force is needed at your school.

Community Allies

When it comes to ending LGBTQ+ bullying, it takes a village. LGBTQ+ students can find allies not just in their schools, but also in their communities. The first place to turn is sympathetic parents. If your parents or your friends' parents are part of your support system, ask them to join the PTA if they aren't already members. A few supportive voices on the PTA could be a great help. People with no kids in school can be natural allies. Public schools are funded by local taxpayers. A local business that is run by LGBTQ+ people or LGBTQ+-friendly people might be willing to help students make their case to city council members and others who carry weight in the community. The same tactics used with the school administration and school board—making a good case based on both emotion and data, listening to other points of view, being willing to negotiate—will also help secure support from your community.

When speaking at Temple Israel in 1965, Martin Luther King Jr. said, "The arc of the moral universe is long, but it bends toward justice." The arc of current events is moving toward justice for LGBTQ+ people. LGBTQ+ kids deserve to go to schools free from bullying. With help from allies, they can make it happen.

GLOSSARY

ALLY A person who supports another person and cooperates with them to achieve a larger goal.

BYLAWS A set of rules or policies that govern the members of a club or organization.

CONCESSION Something granted in response to a demand, especially in arguments or negotiations.

CONSCIOUSNESS-RAISING Making people more aware of social and political issues.

CONSTITUTIONAL RIGHT A freedom or liberty that is guaranteed by the Constitution.

CRITERIA A standard or set of guidelines used for judging or comparing one thing to another.

DIPLOMACY The practice of conducting negotiations with the intent of minimizing conflict.

EXTRACURRICULAR Outside of the regular course of study at school.

GENDER The social and cultural habits and practices typically associated with a given sex.

LEGISLATION The body of laws pertaining to a given issue.

LIAISON A person who acts as a go-between to enhance communication between people or groups.

MIGRATE To move from one place or state to another.

NEGOTIATE To work together with other parties to come to an agreement.

NORMALIZE To make something, as an idea or practice, a usual practice.

OVERZEALOUS To be overly eager for a given outcome.

PODIUM A raised platform where someone stands to give a speech or address an audience.

POLICIES The guidelines and rules that determine the practices of an organization.

RHETORIC Language meant to persuade or convince.

TAUNT To insult with the intent of producing anger or humiliation.

VIOLATE To ignore, disregard, or disrespect someone or something.

American Civil Liberties Union
125 Broad Street, 18th Floor
New York, NY 10001
(212) 549-2500
Website: http://www.aclu.org
The ACLU is dedicated to defending and protecting the constitutional rights of individuals.

Egale Canada Human Rights Trust
185 Carlton Street
Toronto, ON M5A 2K7
Canada
(888) 204-7777
Website: http://www.egale.ca
The Egale Canada Human Rights Trust works to support
LGBTQ human rights for Canadian citizens.

Gay Lesbian and Straight Education Network (GLSEN)
110 William Street, 30th Floor
New York, NY 10038
(212) 727-0135
Website: http://www.glsen.org
GLSEN works to make sure all students—regardless of sexual
orientation, gender identity, or gender expression—feel safe,
valued, and respected in school.

GSA Network
1611 Telegraph Avenue, Suite 1002

Oakland, CA 94612
(415) 552-4229
Website: http://gsanetwork.org
The GSA Network is a national network of Gay-Straight Alliance
    groups that empowers and trains LGBTQ+ youth to create
    safer schools and healthier communities.

LGBT Youthline
P.O. Box 73118 Wood Street PO
Toronto, ON M4Y 2W5
Canada
(800) 268-9688
Website: http://www.youthline.ca
The LGBT Youthline provides LGBTQ+ peer-to-peer support
    for Canadian youth.

Teaching Tolerance
400 Washington Avenue
Montgomery, AL 36104
(888) 414-7752
Website: http://www.splcenter.org/teaching-tolerance
A project of the Southern Poverty Law Center, Teaching
    Tolerance is dedicated to combatting prejudice among youth
    and promoting equality, inclusiveness, and equitable learning
    environments in the classroom.

The Trevor Project
PO Box 69232

West Hollywood, CA 90069
(866) 488-7386
Website: http://www.thetrevorproject.org
The Trevor Project provides help to LGBTQ+ youth in crisis,
    including suicide prevention services.

Websites

Because of the changing nature of internet links, Rosen
Publishing has developed an online list of websites related to the
subject of this book. This site is updated regularly. Please use this
link to access the list:

http://www.rosenlinks.com/LGBTQG/bully

FOR FURTHER READING

Bazelon, Emily. *Sticks and Stones: Defeating the Culture of Bullying and Rediscovering the Power of Character and Empathy*. New York, NY: Random House, 2014.

Belge, Kathy, and Marke Bieschke. *Queer: The Ultimate LGBT Guide for Teens*. San Francisco, CA: Zest, 2011.

Ellis, Deborah. *We Want You to Know: Kids Talk About Bullying*. Regina, Saskatchewan: Cocteau, 2011.

Gay, Kathlyn. *Activism: The Ultimate Teen Guide*. Lanham, MD: Rowman and Littlefield, 2016.

Huegel, Kelly. *GLBTQ: The Survival Guide for Gay, Lesbian, Bisexual, Transgender, and Questioning Teens*. Golden Valley, MN: Free Spirit Publishing, 2011.

Kaushik, Bhavya, and Ann Jamieson, eds. *The Bullied Anthology: Stories of Success*. Lansdale, PA: Reading Harbor, 2015.

Lehmann, Raychelle Cassada, et al. *The Bullying Workbook for Teens: Activities to Help You Deal with Social Aggression and Cyberbullying*. Oakland, CA: Instant Help, 2013.

Mardell, Ashley. *The ABCs of LGBT*. Coral Gables, FL: Mango, 2016.

Pohlen, Jerome. *Gay & Lesbian History for Kids: The Century-Long Struggle for LGBT Rights*. Chicago, IL: Chicago Review Press, 2016.

Savage, Dan, and Terry Miller. *It Gets Better: Coming Out, Overcoming Bullying, and Creating a Life Worth Living*. New York, NY: Plume, 2012.

Short, Donn. *Don't Be So Gay! Queers, Bullying, and Making Schools Safe*. Vancouver, BC: UBC Press, 2014.

Thompson, Laurie Ann. *Be a Changemaker: How to Start Something That Matters*. New York, NY: Simon Pulse, 2014.

BIBLIOGRAPHY

American Academy of Pediatrics. "Gay, Lesbian, and Bisexual Teens: Facts for Teens and Their Parents." Retrieved September 2016. https://www.healthychildren.org/English/ages-stages/teen/dating-sex/Pages/Gay-Lesbian-and-Bisexual-Teens-Facts-for-Teens-and-Their-Parents.aspx.

American Civil Liberties Union. "Harassment and Bullying." Retrieved September 2016. https://www.aclu.org/issues/lgbt-rights/lgbt-youth/harassment-and-bullying.

Bazelon, Emily. "How to Stop the Bullies." *The Atlantic*, March 2013. http://www.theatlantic.com/magazine/archive/2013/03/how-to-stop-bullies/309217.

Centers for Disease Control and Prevention. "Youth Risk Behavior Surveillance System, 2013." Retrieved September 2016. http://www.cdc.gov/healthyyouth/data/yrbs/index.htm.

The Economist. "So Far So Fast: Marriage Equality in America." October 11, 2014. http://www.economist.com/newsbriefing/21623671-week-americas-supreme-court-dealt-supporters-gay-marriage-great-victory-we-look.

Gay, Lesbian & Straight Education Network. *2013 School Climate Survey: The Experiences of Lesbian, Gay, Bisexual and Transgender Youth in Our Nation's Schools.* Retrieved September 2016. http://www.glsen.org/sites/default/files/2013%20National%20School%20Climate%20Survey%20Full%20Report_0.pdf.

Kann, Laura, et al. "Sexual Identity, Sex of Sexual Contacts, and Health-Related Behaviors Among Students in Grades 9-12—United States and Selected Sites, 2015." Centers for Disease

Control and Prevention. Retrieved October 2016. https://www.cdc.gov/mmwr/volumes/65/ss/ss6509a1.htm.

King, Martin Luther, Jr. "Sermon at Temple Israel at Hollywood." February 26, 1965. http://www.americanrhetoric.com/speeches/mlktempleisraelhollywood.htm.

McCarthy, Justin. "Satisfaction with Acceptance of Gays in U.S. at New High." Gallup, January 18, 2016. http://www.gallup.com/poll/188657/satition-acceptance-gays-new-high.aspx.

McGill, Andres. "Americans Are Embracing Transgender Rights." *The Atlantic*, August 25, 2016. http://www.theatlantic.com/politics/archive/2016/08/americans-are-embracing-transgender-rights/497444.

Miller, Hayley. "How to Be an LGBT Ally." Human Rights Campaign, October 7, 2015. http://www.hrc.org/blog/how-to-be-an-lgbt-ally.

NoBullying.com. "LGBT Bullying Statistics." Retrieved October 2016. https://nobullying.com/lgbt-bullying-statistics.

Pohlen, Jerome. *Gay & Lesbian History for Kids: The Century-Long Struggle for LGBT Rights.* Chicago, IL: Chicago Review Press, 2016.

Savage, Dan, and Terry Miller. *It Gets Better: Coming Out, Overcoming Bullying, and Creating a Life Worth Living.* New York, NY: Plume, 2012.

Short, Donn. *Don't Be So Gay! Queers, Bullying, and Making Schools Safe.* Vancouver, BC: UBC Press, 2014.

Signorile, Michelangelo. *It's Not Over: Getting Beyond Tolerance, Defeating Homophobia, and Winning True Equality.* New York, NY: Houghton Mifflin Harcourt, 2015.

Silver, Nate. "Change Doesn't Usually Come This Fast." FiveThirtyEight, June 26, 2015. http://fivethirtyeight.com /datalab/change-doesnt-usually-come-this-fast.

Teaching Tolerance. "Best Practices: Creating a LGBT-Inclusive Climate." Retrieved September 2016. http://www.tolerance .org/lgbt-best-practices.

Thompson, Laurie Ann. *Be a Changemaker: How to Start Something That Matters*. New York, NY: Simon Pulse, 2014.

INDEX

A

allies
  in the community, 50–51
  finding, 22–25
  supporting each other, 25, 26
  talking to, 26–28
American Academy of Pediatrics, 22
American Civil Liberties Union (ACLU), 17, 35, 38
asexual, 10

B

bisexual, 10
bullying
  consequences of, 14
  in cyberspace, 12–14
  definition, 8
  kinds of, 11–12
  myths and facts about, 21
  proactively preventing, 17–18
  reporting, 38–40
  standing up to, 15–17
  victims of, 8–9

C

Centers for Disease Control and Prevention (CDC), 6, 9, 12, 14
cisgender, 10
city council, 50
Clinton, Hillary, 6
coming out, 19–20, 26
cyberbullying, 12–14

D

Democratic National Convention (2016), 15
"Don't Ask, Don't Tell," 5

E

Equal Access Act of 1984, 35, 47, 48

F

Facebook, 12, 26

G

Gallup's 2016 Mood of the Nation survey, 22

ABOUT THE AUTHOR

Avery Elizabeth Hurt is a children's book author and journalist who for many years has covered LGBTQ+ issues for publications including *The New Physician* magazine. She worked with the Human Rights Campaign to support marriage equality and is still active in supporting LGBTQ+ rights.

PHOTO CREDITS

Cover, p. 1 Digital Vision/Thinkstock; pp. 4–5 Universal Images Group/Getty Images; p. 9 Phil Boorman/Cultura/Getty Images; p. 11 Image Source/Digital Vision/Getty Images; p. 13 Urilux/E+/Getty Images; p. 16 Fuse/Corbis/Getty Images; p. 18 Amy Sussman/Invision for Armour/AP Images; p. 20 Maskot/Getty Images; p. 23 Pressmaster/Shutterstock.com; p. 24 RosalreneBetancourt 6/Alamy Stock Photo; p. 27 Ezra Bailey/Taxi/Getty Images; p. 29 Dan Dalton/Caiaimage/Getty Images; p. 31 Purestock/Thinkstock; p. 32 goodluz/Shutterstock.com; p. 36 © iStockphoto.com/DMEPhotography; p. 37 Portland Press Herald/Getty Images; p. 41 Johnny Greig/E+/Getty Images; p. 45 Hulton Archive/Archive Photos/Getty Images; p. 48 asiseeit/E+/Getty Images; p. 49 ZUMA Press Inc/Alamy Stock Photo; interior pages background (hands) Rawpixel.com/Shutterstock.com.

Designer: Nelson Sá; Photo Researcher: Karen Huang